MEET MAYA

STORY BY AMY JANE LOEB
ILLUSTRATED BY ANNA HOFFMAN

For My Mother

Everytime I read a story, I hear your voice in me. Now, Maya will be a story that we share forever. Thank you for your support every step of the way. We love you very much.

And The Loeb Family

For teaching me everything there was to know about dogs, including how to treat them as part of the family and love them unconditionally. Special thanks to my Aunt Pauline for all of the care you provide to the world, and to dogs, and to me. The world is a better place with you in it.

And for everyone who has known Maya and loved her for her strengths.

Maya is a rescue dog. When her owner rescued her from the side of the road, she didn't know what to expect.

1

Fortunately, Maya has lots of great qualities. She can run very fast and jump really high!

She loves to fetch balls. She'll jump high into the air and catch them with her mouth no matter which direction they go. Then she'll bring the ball back to her owner and want to do it all over again!

Maya is also a very good listener and follows her owner everywhere that she goes. They have hiked all over the country together!

But sometimes Maya has funny behaviors.

When Maya meets someone unfamiliar, she might growl or bark.

When Maya hears loud noises, she often runs and hides.

And sometimes Maya will stop and FREEZE in response to scary things!

Her owner began to wonder why Maya acts differently, and she realized that Maya wasn't treated very nicely before she was rescued.

This got her owner thinking about how sometimes this happens to people too.

How we treat one another matters a lot. When someone is mistreated, it can stick with them and lead to them acting funny just like Maya: freezing, fighting or running away.

Her owner decided to learn more about how to help people who have been through something tough.

What Maya's owner learned is that you can never know how someone's past has impacted them. It may lead them to act differently during times of stress, just like Maya does.

The most important thing that we can do is to be kind to one another.

We can also focus on the good qualities that people have rather than their funny behaviors.

And make sure to take plenty of walks!

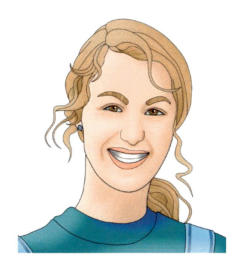

MEET THE ARTIST
ANNA IS A FREELANCE ARTIST ORIGINATING FROM DENMARK.
YOU CAN FIND HER ART ON INSTAGRAM
@SOMETIMES.ANNA.MAKES.ART

Made in the USA
Middletown, DE
24 February 2024

50164414R00022